CAREF

THE ABC'S OF CAREER PREPARATION
JIM WESTMORELAND
RELEASE DATE: AUG. 20, 2021

A manual presents the basics of career advancement.

Career specialist Westmoreland here presents a second edition of his book on all aspects of job seeking and advancement. He arranges his advice under alphabetical headings—A is for "Apprehensive About Starting?"; G is for "Gathering Information and the Internet"; T is for "To Keep a Job, Make Time for Yourself." The arrangement is loose and flexible, designed in an intentionally modular way so that readers can jump around to whichever sections most directly address their specific needs. This approach is enhanced by Westmoreland's decision to fill his relatively short manual with many interactive features, boxes, charts, and checklists that readers are encouraged to fill in themselves. Each of the book's sections concludes with insights in bold type—summaries and distillations of everything that's been outlined. The maxims include "A truly educated person may be the one who can carry on a conversation with anyone about anything," and "If you criticize a lot of things, then first take time to be critical of yourself." As these maxims show, Westmoreland tends to present high school platitudes as though they were profundities. But this author is so insightful when it comes to work situations, particularly management, that readers will overlook being told things like "No one likes to work where their work is never quite good enough." Westmoreland is direct in assessing the nuances of management and communication, although even here he can't always resist the urge to deliver obvious bromides like "Just because you have knowledge of something, do not expect everyone to know or understand it." The result is an accessible and conversational motivation manual that deftly clarifies a process that even experienced job seekers can find overwhelming.

A straightforward, useful, and richly interactive guide to all aspects of job seeking.

—**Kirkus Review**

Pub Date: Aug. 20, 2021
ISBN: 978-1984532107
Page Count: 86
Publisher: Xlibris US
Review Posted Online: Nov. 22, 2021

cAREER BASICs

The ABC's of Career Preparation

DR. JIM WESTMORELAND

For those searching for a satisfying career
For any job searchers

Second printing from the original *ABC's of Career Preparation*

Library of Congress Control Number:		2018906875
ISBN:	Hardcover	978-1-9845-3210-7
	Softcover	978-1-9845-3211-4
	eBook	978-1-9845-3212-1

To order additional copies of this book, contact:
Xlibris
844-714-8691
www.Xlibris.com
Orders@Xlibris.com
775722

CONTENTS

This book is dedicated to wonderful mentors for me… I learned about career choices by their good examples and from conversations and a relationship based on trust and respect…

Furney James …served as the Director of Career Services and was among the most encouraging humans I have ever met….

Florence Weaver… a teacher and friend who encouraged me through the Doctoral Program

Xlibris, Thank you to your staff for work with my book so many will have better opportunities from using this as a tool.

If this booklet is discovered and you find it, then please return it to the *name below.*

If you find it and like what it is saying or know someone who could benefit from it, please tell them where they could get a copy.

If you might know of a job for the owner below since you see from the written answers that much thought has been given, then please share.

SIGN YOUR FULL NAME _____

How business like is your signature?

PRINT NAME _____

Present Address	**Permanent Address**
_____	_____
_____	_____
Phone _____	**Phone** _____
Email _____	**Email** _____

> Dedicated to family, friends, and
> coworkers with whom I have had the
> pleasure to learn about work *and* life.

Having earned a Doctorate in Education with the focus on training and development, the author worked with students and employers daily in a university career services office and received a Master's degree in Counselor Education and another Master's degree in Adult Education. Later he served as Associate Dean in the largest and second longest AACSB accredited business school in North Carolina. The first printing was created so others could use and was made available through many bookstores and school systems so that more people will learn about:

The ABC's of Career Preparation © 1983 J. R. Westmoreland

cAreer BasiCs © 1996 James R. Westmoreland

START YOUR SEARCH HERE

SEARCHING FOR WORK can be fun if you understand when to start and if you start early enough.

If you like challenges, then enjoy learning more about this exciting process.

> I believe in simplicity.
> Use this easy-to-follow
> guide and skip the parts
> that you do not need.

Most People Do Not Know How to Look for Work

If you use this workbook, then you will be better prepared *than the majority* of job seekers. Many career aids may be similar, but in this booklet, you can direct and choose what *you* want to learn. Many will find work without making a résumé or having a formal interview; however, all these ideas can be helpful to consider.

Job Hunting Skills Can Be Learned

There are some fundamentals you can work on to help you prepare to be the best person for a specific job. Many of your personality traits *and* learned skills will combine to determine whether or not you will be selected. The job you get will be the result of the groundwork you have done over time and may be more of who you are.

Your Career Development

So often, headlines with UNEMPLOYMENT appear and show how many people are not working. When you look at the overall picture though, one can see how many individuals are really being productive members of society through voluntary contributions or other work efforts. For anyone with or without a job, he or she must recognize that *there are always* things that can be done to make progress in their *own career development* process.

From *experiences* in aiding individuals in their career decisions,
From *opportunities* to learn about career considerations from others,
and
From many *observations* about life planning,
this simplified version of short statements
about the job search is offered
with the hopes that they might
inspire you to consider new possibilities,
encourage you to develop better job search skills, and help you
appreciate the best of what you know,
what you already have, and
what you *will* have in the future.

THIS IS YOURS TO USE AND MARK IN AS YOU SEE FIT!

INTRODUCTION TO CAREER BASICS—
THE ABC'S OF CAREER PREPARATION

THIS IS NOT to mislead you to believe that career planning is as easy as ABC. It is designed to show the *process* involved.

My goal is to present all that follows in a format that you will find easy-to-use!

As anyone

Begins to look for a job, he or she

Can certainly

Do some things to

Enable himself or herself to be better prepared.

For that individual, there are some

Guidelines that can be followed.

He or she could first read this booklet.

In reviewing one's strengths, a suitable

Job might be discovered. By

Keeping a positive attitude and

Looking in appropriate ways, friends

Might be found who will help

Negate fears about *searching for work* as they

Offer advice and encouragement. You may also

Prepare a résumé of your background so your

Qualities can best be shown to help sell yourself.

Reflecting upon your strengths in this way

Should help better prepare you for interviews.

Tips on interviewing are also given and

Under each letter of the alphabet, you can

View various elements of career planning.

Whether you want to work as an

X-ray technician or in business,

You can read this discussion of A to

Z considerations, which now follows.

cAreer BasiCs

THE ABC'S OF CAREER PREPARATION

Chapters

A

APPREHENSIVE ABOUT STARTING?

Attributes, Attitudes

**Your
Career
Choice**

Chocolate or vanilla ice cream? Blue or red? Are you wondering what this has to do with career choices? We are always making decisions and choices, some obviously more significant than others. As you go through this booklet, you will have some choices to make. You can best learn about yourself and your career if you complete most of the sections.

**What
Decisions
Have You
Made?**

Do you have a geographical preference where you want to live and work?

☐ No preference

☐ Desired places_____

Type of position if known already:

☐ _____

☐ Unknown

**Decisions
Can
Actually
Help One
See More
Options!**

What can you do now?	—DECISION	Explore more careers.	—DECISION→	Read more about . . .
		Be satisfied with what you are doing now.		Talk with someone . . .
				Write for more information.

Attributes   How do you feel about yourself? Before you can really begin to reach your goals and if your search is to be a worthwhile effort, then you must feel pretty good about yourself. By first recognizing your *strengths, accomplishments,* and *attributes* through the following sections, you can better focus on your possibilities and get some good clues about your future. If your life is in order and you know your pluses, then doors will probably be easily opened.

Attitudes   A *positive attitude* will be most important for you to continue. To whom have you been supportive lately? You will be looking to others for assistance, so you should be ready and able to help those with whom you deal daily.

STOP . . . This booklet is designed so you can stop here or any page and read more at your next opportunity if you choose.

Those who seem to have the most "luck" in landing a job are generally those who have done their career preparation throughout their daily activities. They have learned how to explore and plan as they live.

B

BEGINNING—BEING YOUR BEST

Where and how do I start?

> **The two biggest questions of most job seekers are**
> *Where do I start?* **and** *How do I start?*

Where and How Do I Start? If these are your first questions, then this alphabetic guide should help you as you take time to review it. The question of *when* you should start should also be considered because whatever your present employment or school standing is, it is important to *learn how to start and look* now.

Why Now?

1. If you are a student or presently secure in a job, you are not an imminent threat to anyone's job. You are in a better position to *explore* and test *your possibilities.*
2. It will be much easier to *evaluate all* your *opportunities* if you start soon enough before graduation or the end of a job or when you desperately need work.
3. If you do not start until you graduate or end a job, you may have the dilemma of turning down your first offer while needing time to consider other offers. You may also appear *desperate!*

What Is It You Want in Life?

Can you indicate *two* of the choices below that you most desire (even better if you rank them?

____ Money	____ Freedom	____ Good health
____ Success	____ Satisfying work	____ Adequate housing
____ Security	____ Recognition	

People
You
Admire

Another way to determine your career possibilities can be done by having you write in the following blanks the names of two working people you admire:

_____   _____

Qualities

Please check the (or rank the top five) qualities that you observe in these persons:

___ Honest   ___ Good communicator

___ Powerful   ___ Good provider

___ Creative   ___ Good manager

___ Flexible   ___ Sense of humor

___ Positive   ___ Rich monetarily

___ Sensitive   ___ Spiritual

___ Appreciated   ___ Has much freedom

___ Intense   ___ Genuine

This might be used later in a section where you describe yourself.

Being
Your
Best!

Despite how the media and society encourage us to be number 1, not everyone can be number 1 in the world, the universe, in your neighborhood, or in your family. Being straightforward, honest, and comfortable in your daily dealings with others will make better things happen for you.

You do help identify your own values by what you admire in others.

Sometimes you cannot see the depth of a person from the pier, you may need to wade in a little.

C

CAREFUL THOUGHT AND PLANNING

What could you do?

Jobs with a Future
After reflecting upon *one's own* skills, talents, and potential, one might also consider the happenings of the world and their influence on his or her career choice. Being aware of society's impact and of the changing economic conditions can help one see the *most realistic* options possible. To stop pursuing a position or job in the field that you most enjoy because of overcrowding may not be the thing to do. *You* may be one of the best persons around to handle that type of responsibility.

Population Changes
There will be many types of jobs in the future that do not even exist now. When baby booms happened, suppliers of babies' needs have been profitable; when fewer babies are born, manufacturers have had to make necessary adjustments in their product lines. Jobs that support an aging population should be considered by those thinking ahead.

Role Changes
Changes in society have opened up job opportunities for both sexes more than ever. The changes for childcare needs will certainly affect many people's career decisions.

Economic Conditions
In a tight economy, people hold on to their jobs longer and less entry-level jobs are available. One needs to maintain an optimistic attitude with a realistic approach to all decisions.

Can You Balance?

 *Concern for self*   *Concern for others*

One must recognize the balance between these two areas as they choose their careers. If the scale is tilted too much either way, then one's opportunities will be limited.

Jobs vs. Careers

Your *job* may help you pay your bills. However, your choice of a *career* field will determine your lifestyle.

Happy People

As people decide or evolve into their careers, the happiest people seem to be the ones who have learned to *explore* as they live *and* those who *learn from all they encounter.*

Please check or rank any of the following that you could enjoy or envision yourself doing:

__ Studying the need for a product	__ Preparing a product
__ Producing a product	__ Packaging the product
__ Designing a product	__ Deciding on how many to produce
__ Managing the product	__ Teaching people how to use
__ Delivering the product	__ Checking to see if it safe to use

---

Take time to know a seventy-year-old person and a five-year-old. If you do not, then you will miss out on a lot of wisdom and perspective and a lot of honesty and frankness.

D

DISCUSS WITH OTHERS

Decision-Making

If you are undecided about a career *or* if you are changing jobs, then consider how to avoid making snap decisions.

1. Ask a friend "how can I prepare and also allow sufficient time to make an educated decision?"

2. Starting in an appropriate way may be the hardest part of the process when making any decision. Some objective self-evaluation can first help show what direction you should take. Choose those who offer advice very carefully. Everyone can have an opinion, but you can get another's through their lenses of experiences.

3. When you *look ahead to future changes* or if you anticipate opportunities, you can begin to lay a good *foundation* toward a satisfying career.

Someone Who is the person with whom you can typically sit and discuss
with whom important things about yourself? Who is someone with whom
you can talk you share some common ground? _____

Just as barriers in forming relationships often result from a lack of things in common, job searchers need to make efforts to establish relationships and recognize commonalities to break down those barriers.

Can You Make an Honest Appraisal of Yourself and Your Talents?	Which of the following describes you? (Check and then rank top 5)		
	__ Creative	__ Powerful	__ Genuine
	__ Hard worker	__ Flexible	__ Good sense of humor
	__ Reserved	__ Sensitive	__ _____
	__ Intense	__ Positive	__ _____

Would you desire a career that is—? (Rank top 2 or 3)		
__ 48 hours a week	__ Mostly outdoor	__ In any geographic area
__ Service to others	__ Physical labor	__ In professional surroundings
__ 35 percent or more travel	__ Computer oriented	__ 40 percent or less paperwork

Check those that you offer an employer.	What have you done to show these qualities?	
__ Good leader	_____	Cite any
__ Good follower	_____	experience
__ Good organizer	_____	that shows
__ Work well with others	_____	these
__ Can follow instructions	_____	for your
__ Can show others how to work	_____	résumé.

For your decisions or goals, can you see two or more options, and can you list the good and bad factors for each choice? If you do this with many of your decisions, you can more easily sort out the pros and cons of almost any choice!

For example		**Your Choice**	
Buying a Car	**Buying a Motorcycle**	**Career in____**	**Or a Career in____**
Pros or Cons	Pros or Cons	Pros or Cons	Pros or Cons
Safer, expensive use all year	More fun, dangerous		

For decisions, write two or more solutions with good & bad for each,
and it will be easier if you can write the options.

E

EXPLORE YOUR FUTURE

Education Hints

How Can You Explore? Just as when you are making the purchase of a big item, you probably look around and ask opinions. In *career selection*, many seem to just float toward or fall into a career. For some, that may be okay and that may happen to you. For your career choice to be a good one though, you probably will have done various things to lay some *groundwork*.

Exploraview "Can you explore and view someone at their work?"	1. Is there someone that you might visit and discuss careers in _____?
	2. Can you visit and ask for ten minutes of their time to ask:
	A. How can I prepare myself for a career in _____?
	B. What can you briefly tell me about your organization?
	C. What are the responsibilities in an entry-level job?
	3. Stick to the ten minutes requested unless they offer more! Read more under sections K and Q.

Two B's or Not Two B's A proven record of a complete *education* can be helpful. Here are some proven ways to get the most out of any educational effort.

1. Try to know *something about* your *teachers.* Where did he or she attend school or grow up? You might have some things in common to add a personal touch and encourage you to work to learn even more.

2. If *teachers know you,* they sometimes unconsciously *direct* their lectures to you to make sure you understand and learn.

3. *Class attendance* may be the key. Let teachers know in advance if you cannot be there. For the one who does not miss a class, a higher letter grade is often received compared to the person who misses two or more classes.

4. *Terms to memorize?* Notecards or cards with a term or question on one side *and* the answer on the other hand can be carried around and reviewed when you have some spare time.

5. Besides the internet, become familiar with the *library*. You may not know everything, but you can know where to find your answers. Many find that they can study better in a study carrel or place that blocks off interference.

6. Do you have any *breaks* in the day after a hard class? Review at that time for your best learning!

7. Learn from *mistakes*. You will probably see the questions again. Falling behind in math, science, or foreign languages will be disastrous, so consider using a calendar to mark or plan your progress.

8. *Memory* is aided by *association*. Just as in remembering someone's name, if you can remember something else about the person (hometown?), then you may have a hook on which to hang other information.

9. Keep a *list* of things to do, prioritize them, and begin.

10. Have a basic *schedule* and allow time for your *needs*—friends, food, exercise, study, and sleep.

A truly educated person may be the one who can carry on a conversation with anyone about anything.

First, find your strengths (many of which are unknown). You will see that you should and can depend on your own abilities.

F

FIGURE OUT YOUR MOST REALISTIC OPTIONS

Possible Career Fields

Endless Choices	The possibilities for future work are almost endless to the one who is open to new ideas—jobs of the future (even those of next year) do not exist now. Some jobs of the past will not exist in the future. One should be aware of the oversupply of workers in certain fields and also recognize that the popular trends of today may overrun the work fields that you hear the most about now.

What Can You Consider Now?	*Summer work* *Part-time work* *Volunteer work* *Internships*	Use these to explore new or desirable fields of work. The *summer* bank teller has improved his or her chances to work in a bank in later years. Start six months ahead to get the best job. Can you volunteer or, even better, observe (see Exploraview in chapter E)?

What Jobs Have You Had?	1. Clerk 2. Sold anything? 3. Worked with the public?	4. Done yard work? 5. Helped in construction or repair work? 6. Babysitter or childcare? 7. _____

What Is It that Makes You Unique? Often past work experiences or exposure to work areas can show your efforts and hopes *better than anything* you say in a job interview. Show your *involvement* in something!

Appreciating your distinctiveness	Have you—? ____ worked on a computer project ____ traveled extensively ____ lived in more than one place ____ worked in any way that is related to your chosen field

Options for Your Future   What do you now have in mind? Help is available through most any library or counselor's office as they can answer the following questions. Someone who works helping others may have resources you may see.

1. Can you describe a possible career choice in a few paragraphs?
2. Do you know its *salary range* or the *basic requirements*?
3. Where can you write for more information about any career?

The career fields below have been designated by the US Office of Education to categorize different areas of work. Take a moment to respond. If you are not sure what the category means but you think you may have done work that is related, then check it.

I have had jobs related to these fields:		I would like to consider or learn more about
_____	Agriculture	_____
_____	Business / Office	_____
_____	Health areas	_____
_____	Public service (Education)	_____
_____	Hospitality / Recreation	_____
_____	Marine / Water-Related	_____
_____	Transportation	_____
_____	Manufacturing	_____
_____	Personal services	_____
_____	Consumer services	_____
_____	Environmental / Science concerns	_____
_____	Communications / Media	_____
_____	Marketing / Distribution / Sales	_____
_____	Construction	_____
_____	Arts / Designing / Performing	_____

G

GATHERING INFORMATION AND THE INTERNET

Where can you look?

While you are in school or while you are employed, you are in the best situation to explore possibilities!

Yes ____ No ____ 1. Can you go to an area where you *might* like to work and get an idea of the actual sights, sounds, and smells of the workplace?

Yes ____ No ____ 2. Can you make time to visit this place in the next two weeks?

Yes ____ No ____ 3. Whom could you talk to, and could you ask them any of the following?

    a. What educational background or other qualities do most of your employees have?

    b. I know a little about your organization, but is there someone who might describe it to me in more detail?

    c. Could you utilize any volunteer services?

How does one get information necessary to prepare themselves for the job search? The following lists the information most people want to know and also includes some of the better sources.

Where can I get information about ____?	Most libraries have these sources, or they can get the resource for you.
Careers, job outlook, training required, where to write for more information	*Occupational Outlook Handbook* by the Government Printing Office
Job titles, descriptions	*Guide for Occupational Exploration*

Job descriptions	http://www.onetonline.org/
Company information, addresses, type of product, listing by location and type of business	*Dun & Bradstreet Million Dollar Directory*
Corporate background and history, stock information, earnings	*Standard & Poor's Reports*
Good information on banks and financial, transportation, utilities, industrial, and international companies	*Moody's Manuals*
Books and pamphlets on books in your possible career choice	Books like *Where to Start* by Rockcastle, M. (editor)
Company whose brand-name product I know but need to know who produces it	Thomas Register of Manufacturing Firms
Addresses and descriptions of manufacturing firms in my state	Most states have tools that list these. For example, Directory of _____ (state) Manufacturing Firms, Virginia Industrial Directory, etc.
Further schooling	Information or catalogs for many schools are online.
Addresses for companies in my area	Use searches—one of the most-used sources of career help.
Other career resources?	Google or first ask your librarian or check your bookstore. Stop by your school counselor's office.

Avoid insinuating to anyone about how they should do their job, unless you are their boss. Even then, a good boss will be clear and direct in his or her expectations.

H

HAVE A RÉSUMÉ READY
(REZ-ZU-MAY)

Some samples and a worksheet

Basics

Follow-Up
Letters or
Thank-You
Notes

Most of the information you will see written about the documents necessary for a job search will focus on the *résumé*. A résumé is a good starting point to let you review your experience, *but* never overlook cover letters and thank-you notes as *equally* important documents.

1. A *résumé* is a document that shows your address, education, work experience, and any other important facts about you. The reader cannot know accurate information unless you offer it clearly.
2. In thirty seconds or less, a reader should be able to know:
   • how to reach you,
   • schooling you have had,
   • the kind of job you would like to have,
   • types of work you have had or that you know how to do, and
   • any accomplishments that show your personality or involvement.
3. A well-balanced layout is vital. It should show your uniqueness without being too fancy.
4. List your most recent education or work first, then follow with other education.
5. Avoid abbreviations. Short descriptive phrases tell it best.
6. Have a friend read it for suggestions about your format and to detect errors.
7. Volunteer-work experience or other significant titles can be put under separate categories. You can make up your own headings. One of the best ways to order has *relevant experience* near the top of your résumé.

8. Whether online or hard copy, all libraries have books with examples of various résumés.

9. Most authorities suggest one-page résumés unless you have a great deal of experience. Copies must be neat and clean—your efforts will probably be wasted if you send a poorly copied résumé.

10. Show *skills, accomplishments,* or *capabilities* as opposed to duties. If you are just sending résumés, you may be doing things out of order (see section J). Could you call or write for information about position titles or the company itself? Can you be sure that you are writing to the correct person?

Advertising You A *résumé* should be considered an *advertisement for you.* Which items online or on TV or in a newspaper catch your attention? Are they those with detailed paragraphs or short messages?

Show How You Can Help Make sure your résumé honestly represents you and tells an employer what they want *and* need to know. It is not a "brag sheet" to list every honor since the first grade but a description of you and a message to the reader about how you can help their organization.

Do not expect people to think as you do.

Do not expect people to do things for you, just accept and appreciate the good things that they do.

SALLY MOST TOOGOOD

PERMANENT ADDRESS	CAMPUS ADDRESS (Until Month Day, Year)
432 Main Street	123 College Street
Hometown, State 43210	Campustown, State 01234
Area Code – Phone	Area Code – Phone
Email	Email

Objective

A position in museum management which utilizes my education and experience

Education

MY FAVORITE UNIVERSITY; Campustown, State _____ Year - May Year

Bachelor of Science in History, Minor: Business Administration Overall Grades: 3.2 on a 4.0 scale, 3.5 in major significant courses including

- Medieval History
- _____
- _____
- _____

    Honors paper on medieval museum record-keeping
    History honor fraternity—Phi Alpha Theta, President Dates/Year
    Intramural basketball and bowling

LOCAL COMMUNITY COLLEGE; Community, State   Year – Year

    Transferred after completing general college transfer courses
    Student-government association legislator
    Volunteer with Red Cross blood drive

OUR TOWN HIGH SCHOOL; Our Town, State   Year – Year

    Outstanding Citizenship Award as a senior
    Pep club, debate team, track team

Work Experience

STATE DEPARTMENT OF   ; Capitol, State Summer of _____

    Internship—studied other state's museum management policies

    Worked as an aide to the state director of museums

HAPPY'S DEPARTMENT STORE; Our Town, State

    Salesperson—Shoe Department; started on loading dock,
    became Leading salesperson over two
    holiday periods   High School and College

TOM'S MANUFACTURING FIRM; Our Town, State

    Stock/Inventory Clerk—developed new inventory system   Summer
    Date/Year

Volunteer Experience

BEAUFORT HISTORICAL REENACTMENT—participate annually in
    this program, Developed full military dress costume of the period

OUR TOWN ARTS COUNCIL—member of Museum Development
    Committee

References

Available upon request.

SEYMOUR B. LOWE

123 Eastover Drive
Anytown, USA 99531
919-555-4321
Messages: 919-555-1234
Email _____

Objective   Desire opportunity to work using my
_____ major and past
work experience as a _____

Qualifications   Proven experience with electrical components
Knowledge of broad range of electrical terms
Sales experience with many types of customers

Education   MY _____ UNIVERSITY; City, State
Bachelor of Science in DISCIPLINE or MAJOR

Minor—Business Administration
Graduation: May Year

Significant Courses included:

- Metals   • Production Techniques

- Graphics   • Construction Principals

Overall Grades: 3.1 on a 4.0 scale, 3.3 in Major

Epsilon Pi Tau—Honorary Industrial
Technology Fraternity

Scott Hall House Council Governing Body

MY FIRST COMMUNITY COLLEGE; Town, State

Associate of Arts in BUSINESS
ADMINISTRATION   Year–Year

Student Government Legislator

Gamma Beta Phi Honorary Scholastic Fraternity

Experience   ELECTRONICS OUTLET; Greenville, State

Part-Time Sales Clerk   September Year to May Year
Assisted customers in selection of
appropriate equipment

CLARK CONSTRUCTION
COMPANY; City, State
Electrician's Assistant   Summer of Year

CJ's DEPARTMENT STORE;
Hometown, United States of America
Sales Clerk   High School and College breaks
Assisted with inventory and sales of men's clothes

HAMBURGER PALACE; Hometown,
United States of America
Cook and Cashier   Summers Year and Year

Personal Data   Born in Welcome, Nebraska, on June 2

Family now lives in Florida

Traveled extensively throughout the United States

Excellent health

Willing to relocate

Available (Month Day Year)

References   Available upon request or from

Professor _____, Associate Professor,
FAVORITE UNIVERSITY Campustown, State Zip

Employer of choice, address
Area Code-Phone   City, State Zip

A RÉSUMÉ GUIDE / WORKSHEET

NAME _____ (ALL CAPITALS)

CAMPUS ADDRESS (or   **PERMANENT ADDRESS**
PRESENT ADDRESS
until May ____)

Street _____   Street _____

City, State, Zip_____   City, State, Zip _____

Area Code-Phone_____   Area Code-Phone _____

OBJECTIVE

Desire to work in _____with the opportunity for increasing responsibilities (Change yours from this example. Some experts even recommend leaving off the objective) _____

EDUCATION

_____COLLEGE:_____, _____, YEAR – YEAR
                     City   State

Bachelor of Science in _____ Minor: _____
Overall Grades: ____._____ on a 4.0 scale, _____._____ in Major

- _____   • _____
- _____   • _____

Honors and Activities
_____, _____ (offices held)
_____ (Significant Projects)

_____HIGH SCHOOL: _____, _____ YEAR___
                        City   State   (Graduated)

Honors and Activities (High school might be used if other areas are limited)_____, _____

EXPERIENCE (Often better if RELEVANT EXPERIENCE before EDUCATION)

_____ PRESENT WORKPLACE: _____, _____
_____ Job Title _____ City   State

PREVIOUS WORKPLACE _____, _____, _____
(Duties here if necessary, say more. For any job, it will explain responsibilities)
Job Title _____   Summers of YEAR

EARLIER WORKPLACE _____; _____
Job Title_____   During High School and college

REFERENCES Available upon request

I

INTERVIEW PREPARATION

Checklist of things to do

**Circle or check items
you know to do.**

_____ 1. Do your homework. There is usually material with which you can be familiar. Can you find out how to pronounce the interviewer's name in advance?

_____ 2. *Dress* as if it were the first day on the job. If you have "exploraviewed" as discussed in section E, then you probably have a good idea what their employees wear.

_____ 3. Be on time; allow extra time even if it means waiting outside. Go by yourself.

_____ 4. Nervous? Having researched a company *or* having visited it or a similar place of employment will give you much more confidence.

_____ 5. When you walk in, *always introduce yourself with your first and last name* and begin with a pleasant greeting or handshake. Saying your name will help the interviewer and encourages the use of your name during the interview. Most interviewers *also* want to impress you; therefore, plan to first talk of your background or things that you have in common.

_____ 6. Be able to present your résumé verbally. Are your remarks direct and clear?

_____ 7. How is your grammar and enunciation? For example, are you from Greenville or "Grainveal," "Nu Yourke," or "Taxes"? Ask a friend about how you say things.

_____ 8. As you sit down, think about your posture and hand movements. Avoid distracting movements. A friend can tell you if you should be concerned. A notebook in your lap may not be as distracting as moving hands. Get something to hold.

_____ 9. Negative remarks or criticism of a former employer is almost sure to knock you out. Interviewers can pick up on this easily from everything you say.

_____ 10. Have at least two copies of your résumé *and* an additional sheet of references ready. The reference sheet should include addresses *and* phone numbers.

_____ 11. The interviewer may already have found the person for the position that you are interviewing; however, what you say might show you are an even better fit into their organization in another capacity.

_____ 12. From the interviewer's perspective
   a. Are you someone they can be proud to bring into the organization?
   b. Would they want to work *with you* on a job?
   Do not judge a company based on that one interviewer!

_____ 13. Show that you can help the employer based on your previous experience. At least show that you are willing to learn and that *you do not know it all.*

_____ 14. Try to have a good idea about the kind of work you would like to do.

_____ 15. Can you talk to people about others who have been most influential in your life? Talk of successes in your life! Talk about your favorite courses. Describe yourself with adjectives. Describe weaknesses and show what you have done to correct them.

_____ 16. Avoid too much makeup, perfume, or cologne.

_____ 17. Try to be the best applicant for your desired job:
   a. Try to think like the employer; get critiqued by other employers you know.
   b. Anticipate questions you might get; write down answers you might give.

_____ 18. Look at the interviewer, not away from their eyes or out the window or around the room.

_____ 19. Learn from your mistakes at places that are not your first choices.

_____ 20. Thank the interviewer for his or her time at the end and by letter.

TOTAL
   0–5 Start again at section A. 11–15 You may get in a door.
   6–10 You'll be able to inquire. 16–20 Probably a good applicant.

JOT DOWN IDEAS FOR YOUR LETTERS

Sample paragraphs and formulas

A résumé by itself is not generally acceptable by most employers; also if all you are doing is sending out résumés, then that may be the reason why you are not employed.

Good business form is essential

123 Eastover Drive
Hometown, State Zip
Month Day, Year

Mr. (Ms.) M. Ployer
Individual's Title
Company or Organization
Address

Avoid "Dear Sir or Madam" Phone or write to get correct name!

Dear Mr. Ployer:

Only a guide, Don't use these same words

Show long term interests... Be sure individuals are held in high regard

    I am writing to inform you that I have submitted an application (or a resume) to the Office of _____ for the position of _____. Having regarded this position as an important one for (reasons). I believe that my background in (of/at)_____.

might fit into an organization like yours.

    Having discussed (or learned about) the responsibilities of this job with _____.

I have also reviewed the progress (development) of your _____. I have been acquainted with these individuals for several years and would be glad for you to ask them about me.

You may just ask for information through this letter

    May I call upon you for an appointment to perhaps discuss my interests (or possible careers in) _____?

I can be reached by phone at 75_____between the hours of 8:00- 9:30 a.m. everyday.

Thank you for your consideration.

Sincerely Yours,

Sign Here

Full Named Typed

If you are not going to followup with thank you notes, do not bother with these

Other paragraphs for different letters:

?	*Use six months before you will be ready to go to work:* I would like the opportunity to meet with you or someone in your firm to learn about careers _____ (majors) in companies like yours. I would appreciate fifteen minutes of your time on any Wednesday or Thursday afternoon.
?	*Do not be deceptive. Only go to learn if they have time. Some may resent this approach if you are out of work or not in school!* I would appreciate a review of my résumé by someone at your _____ (firm) who might guide my job search as I learn about employers who might use my skills.

You will only be limited by your own creativity and imagination.

K

KEEP ADDRESSES AND OTHER DATA CURRENT

Cover all your bases

No one can hire you or help you if they do not
know how or where to locate you!

1. Before starting your job search, you might consider purchasing some postcards or small businesslike note sheets for thank-you notes, just to follow up with administrative assistants or anyone who helps you along the way.

2. Consider keeping a
   1. file or file folder for each job explored,
   2. job index card for each letter you send out or sheet with jobs explored, and
   3. a running document, including places applied.

Some have included the following:

Employer Address	Contact Person	Visited or Researched	Cover Letter and Résumé Sent	Transcripts Sent	Interview
John's Store	John Doe	V—2/2/ Year__	3/1/ Year____	3/30/ Year_____	

Positive Reactions	Negative Considerations	General Notes
Asked for transcripts 3 /29/Year		

3. If your material has been submitted to any office and your phone number or address has changed, then you have the responsibility to let them know of that change.

4. Writing them about a change of address *actually works in your favor.* You will show them that you are responsible enough to maintain your records, *and* you will give them a reason to at least quickly review your information again.

5. Cover your bases. Let people know in a professional way that you are looking for work or employment. You probably should not start mass mailing your résumés to friends and family members, but you can let people know of your hopes. College seniors should be registered with their career services at least two semesters before graduation.

6. There are many sources of career assistance available, and many people who can help send you accurate information. Let your counselors, teachers, or career services or center offices have the most *accurate* and *up-to-date* information they need so that any of the bases might help you. There are many free services available if you just *read* about them. Attend information sessions. You will earn your job by what you have done to be prepared.

Read the parts that you think might help. STOP
whenever you want as you read along.

Do not prepare so much for tomorrow that you miss seeing the beauty of today's sky and the depth of today's people.

Avoid too much detail and try to get a broader perspective as much as possible. Help yourself and others see reasonable completions so to put things at rest.

LETTERS OF RECOMMENDATION AND REFERENCES

How do you describe yourself?

____ 1. It is proper to ask someone before you list them as a reference. (If they are called, then they can give a better first reaction to anyone who asks further questions about you.)

____ 2. If you are asking someone to write a letter of recommendation or fill out some forms for you, consider giving them a copy of your résumé. It might remind them of some experiences that you have had that they might endorse and support.

____ 3. How would you write your own letter of recommendation? Try this:

Dear Employer,

I would like to _____ a. highly recommend
_____ b. recommend
_____ c. say I know

this _____ a. outstanding individual
_____ b. unbelievable
_____ c. unknown

In our dealings, I have found _____ to be __ a. open and honorable
(Name)
__ b. willing to give the extra
__ c. able to follow instructions
__ d. hard to understand

Based on this person's __ a. excellent   class (work) attendance,
__ b. mediocre
__ c. poor

I can __ a. heartily   commend his (her) __ a. fine qualities
__ b. hardly   __ b. questionable

Please feel free to call me for any further information.

____ 4. Have you written thank-you notes to those who wrote you letters of reference, and will you write and tell them when you get a job?

____ 5. Rate yourself according to:

	Superior	Average	Needs Improvement
Grooming			
Attitude			
Punctuality			
Positiveness			
Dependability			
Trustworthiness			
Knowledge of subject			

The best friend is one whom you never have to impress.

M

MOTIVATION AND MODELS

Who supports you?

**What Do
You Want
and Why?**

*Check the
appealing
aspects of a
job that you
hope for!*

____Personal satisfaction in work
____Opportunity to help others
____Chance to deal with people
____Should be able to work at own pace
____Should be appreciated for the work done
____Be able to provide for my needs
____and those of another
____Respected profession
____Anticipated income
____Comfortable lifestyle
____Should never hunger or thirst
____Mistakes will be forgiven
____Able to keep a clear conscience
____Peaceful life
____Responsibility for your own directions
____Freedom

**What is
important in
your life?**

A career by itself will not likely fill all the needs and wants that you might hope for. You might reflect on these three thoughts and how they pertain to you:

—If you have had *someone appreciate* you without expecting anything in return, then you can search for jobs and careers with much more freedom.

—If *you* are able to listen and *appreciate* someone without expecting anything in return, then you might find even more happiness and joy.

—If the *two ideas* above occur at the same time, then there may be no limit to your hopes and dreams.

Challenges   Hopefully you can continue to muster the good attitude required by those looking for employment. If you see this as a *challenge*, then you might find it easier to *ask questions*!

YOU CAN *BE PERSISTENT* WITHOUT BEING *OBNOXIOUS*.

Models   Who are yours? Whose name did you write in section B as a person you admire? You have, hopefully, begun to see the whole *career-preparation process* and reflect that your actual job exploration started years ago with everyone with whom you have interacted. A favorite teacher, neighbor, boss, or friend may be your guide mark for excellence.

Unless you have had the identical role MODELS as someone else, do not have the same expectations for their behavior as yours.

My most generous and caring friends have come forth in ways that I could not have alone controlled. You might also observe that those who truly care about you probably love you and care about you despite what you do. Offer friendship or just a smile to start.

Do not expect everyone to appreciate you. You can never know what anyone brings to a situation.

N

NETWORKING OR ONLINE ADS—OTHER REAL SOURCES

Why people get hired

Technical Backgrounds   For the person with specific skills, listings on the internet and want ads sometimes help. For the person who wants to take a chance on some temporary job, the want ads might also provide an opportunity. However, for the person with a general education, reading this pamphlet with particular emphasis on sections E, G, and Q might help more.

Assume You Are the Employer   Which way would you find people to work in your business?

____ A. Put ad in newspaper or list online

____ B. Ask friends or colleagues

____ C. Take applications continually

____ D. Try to keep in mind people most suited for your firm

a.   If you answered A, then you might expect broad coverage of your opening, but you will probably generate mail from many unqualified individuals. Many are required to advertise even though they have often already found the person who best fits all aspects of their needs.

b.   If you answered B, then you are relying on the memory of others to help you come up with some good candidates. If you ask around, you may generate some false hopes, depending on how your friends promote or describe the opening. This often works well though if you have just one position to fill.

HELP WANTED

c. C certainly generates a lot of paperwork and data but allows the employer a way out of hiring some people. If applications are continually taken, then it sometimes requires an employer to do a lot of follow up to see if persons have already been hired. Applications can be filed away and be available if needed.

d. Most employers like to anticipate future needs, and therefore, stay on the lookout for potentially outstanding employees. If you have done your homework and learned about an employer and what they do, then you have an improved chance to be that outstanding employee most suited for an employer. Of course, you want to know why some people get hired.

Reasons Some People Get Hired

1. Impressive résumés
2. Proven experience
3. Clear expectations
4. Long-term interest in field
5. Good personality—they are considerate!
    (People often must *learn* what that is.)
6. Flexibility
7. Understandable motivation (You can see why they want job.)
8. Enthusiastic about work
9. They seem to speak or look like they fit the job
10. They have met the right people *over time* (This is not just the old "who you know" phrase but "how you know.")

When we help each other, are we not, in fact, helping ourselves?

O

OTHER REASONS PEOPLE
DO NOT GET HIRED

We could not choose you because

Dear Applicant: We received your request for employment, but are sorry to inform you that we are not interested at this time because

Check if any could have ever applied to you.

__ 1. No jobs are open.

__ 2. We are not sure what you want.

__ 3. We are not sure what you can do.

__ 4. You left off information that we need to know:

    __ incomplete addresses (no zip code); no phone

    __ blanks left empty, we could not guess (n/a for "not applicable" would have been better)

    __ everything said, "See résumé." We want to see it on the application.

__ 5. You had a poor cover letter—misspelled words, incorrect grammar, and punctuation.

__ 6. It seems that you just got our company name from some directory and sent it to human resources manager; therefore, it appears that

    __ no research has been done to show that you know anything about our organization;

    __ the person you wrote has not been with us in five years;

    __ we have too many applicants who know a lot more about our organization with similar experiences as your résumé indicates.

__ 7. Your training does not fit at all with our needs.

___ 8. Your grades do not fit our expectations of performance.

___ 9. We saw no involvement in any of your past schooling (we can use good followers as well as good leaders).

___ 10. An application in pencil is rarely accepted.

When you arrived for your interview, you were

___ 1. Five minutes late,
___ 2. Dressed for a dance, not at all like the persons in our organization
___ 3. Nervous, but that is expected; why were you so pushy?
___ 4. I thought I was supposed to interview you; I only spoke a few words,
___ 5. Critical of former employers; your criticism scared me away,
___ 6. Not able to describe favorite courses or professors,
___ 7. Unable to show any experiences that point
    out good communication skills,
___ 8. Too full of excuses for past situations,
___ 9. Not able to show enough flexibility to work, and
___ 10. Not appreciative of my time that I took as an interviewer. I
    never heard from you afterward through a thank-you note!

When you are able to do the following, you may make a fine employee:

___ 1. Show some planning of your career.
___ 2. Identify a few goals.
___ 3. Show why you want to work for someone.
___ 4. Answer questions about yourself.

If there is a round void in your life or career,
then do not try to force in a square peg.

Just because you recognize someone, do not assume they
remember you. Offer your name as you greet them.

P

PERSONAL APPEARANCE
AND POSITIVE ATTITUDE

Your unlimited potential

Finding the Appropriate Look Realistically, one can see that some applications are chosen because they seem to fit the *look and style* of a particular organization. This is not to say that someone should change their look to be chosen, but one should at least consider whether or not this will be an important factor in the selection process.

DRESSING AS IF IT WERE THE FIRST DAY OF WORK is a safe way to prepare. If you have visited the place of employment, then you have some idea of what people will be wearing.

Your Look? Shoes—are they appropriate, neat, and clean?
Hair—many women put their hair up to get a professional look; however, you must feel comfortable though!
Very dark outfits or pale greens are usually not appropriate; neither would be the white Sunday knit dress.

Positive Attitude
- Is it coincidental that those who find employment are usually those with a positive attitude and a self-confident way of doing things?
- People like to be around others who are productive and happy. Those people generally exude confidence.
- Some people need to find negative in anything! Look for what is right about something and let the person who is responsible know you recognize their efforts.
- Those who treat others as if they know it all and could always do a task better will soon make many uncomfortable.

- The really smart person often holds back his or her comments; when they do talk, you will probably be able to learn something significant.
- You never know who might be listening to any negative comments that you might be saying.
- Do not try to solve everyone's problems or weaknesses; the time may be first spent on your own.

Potential You have *unlimited potential* that you will not likely ever fully discover. Try to see the potential in someone that no one else has seen. If you have a gift to do this, use it to bring out the best in others. Most people will never know what they are capable of.

Some will be satisfied with what they are, and that will be okay as they can be happy in their own world.

Give people a little honest and sincere encouragement, and they will prosper.

Three of the best things you can do for people will be to

1. Show them their strengths,

2. Help them develop good self-concept, and

3. Model for them a positive attitude.

Q

QUALIFIED? QUESTIONS YOU CAN ASK

For second interviews

Basic Qualifications Do you meet the basic qualifications for a job? If you are now asking "How can I find out the requirements for a job?" then

Use Your Best Judgment to Determine the Most Appropriate Person

1. Is there anyone whom you might ask about the minimum qualifications?
2. Your chances are improved if you can seek specific job titles that they might have.
3. Can you find out about the background of the persons who have previously held the job?
4. Have you filled out the application first so they can know something about you?
   a. Try to take applications home, so you have more time to neatly and accurately complete the information that is requested.
   b. If there are duplicate forms, then do not shortchange one.
   c. Complete details of dates worked, etc. If *salary history* is requested and there are extenuating circumstances, then some employers may accept the response "Would prefer to discuss in person" in that blank.

Questions You Might Ask NEVER MAKE THE INTERVIEWER UNCOMFORTABLE WITH TOO MANY QUESTIONS OR BY SHARING TOO MUCH OF YOUR KNOWLEDGE ABOUT THE COMPANY TOO SOON.

Often, offers will be made to people who do not realize that they have ever been interviewed. Hopefully, you can get many of your answers from the preparation that you do. When you ask questions, then first recognize *what position* the person whom you ask has in the organization. The following may also be used in *second interviews* if appropriate.

1. Let the person *first* know who you are and why you are there.	Be trustworthy!
2. What are some of the most interesting aspects of this job? May I ask how you got started with_____ (firm?)	Shows interest, interviewer might reflect
3. What qualities might a good candidate possess?	May give you an idea of what is expected
4. What kind of responsibilities does this job have? What would a typical day be like?	You might find out what training might be necessary
5. What are the people doing now who have previously held this position? (This is much better than "What opportunities *will I have* to advance?"	Have they left this kind of work or have they been promoted?
6. What are some of the advantages (and disadvantages) of working with _____? (firm)	BE CAREFUL with this one; interviewer must feel at ease with you.
7. Most say that it is inappropriate to ask about salary in a first interchange. You should first show interest in the employing organization.	Few will offer figures for you in your first contacts.

You can make observations about the people you see at the employer's site. Do not expect all to be like the interviewer and do not be swayed by your first contact with the organization.

R

REFLECTION AND REJECTION

Most Will Experience Both

Rejections   If one can learn from rejections, then those reflections can be one of the most important parts of a job search. Rejections are going to happen to most people, but each can allow us to clarify our goals and become more realistic about what real and best opportunities might be.

HOW DO YOU DEAL WITH REJECTION? While some say that they have never had to fill out an application or had an interview for a job, most have experienced *rejection* in some way. Most can learn what is really expected by employers and the traits that the employers are *really* looking for from the applicants by preparing as discussed in sections E and O.

1. It may be that the person chosen had been known previously by the hiring group. Many employers value the insight and confidence in their choice if they have firsthand knowledge of one's background. Whether it is best or not, some employers can be swayed to hire someone if they believe they are making many other coworkers happier.

2. "Are you just too smooth or too overpowering?" You may come on too strong and threaten those with whom you talk about the job.

3. Is it possible that it is just not in the cards? The job you hope for may not be yours because of internal pressures. The best qualified on paper may not be hired.

4. Those intangibles of personality or "how one deals with others" may be the determining factors. It might be that someone is *in line* for the job, based on their experience and training in a subordinate role.

5. Have you done something where your loyalty might be questioned? Those who play politics may initially win, but more often, they lose out over time.
6. Do you fit the image that is expected? This may be the most unfair reason for one not to get a job if they are truly the best qualified. However, *if* this is the reason for rejection, *then* you will probably be better off somewhere else.

Reflection   Do not just go to interview for practice *but do* test the waters in some safe spots where you can learn as you begin to look for your best place of employment. It might be best to try smaller places first to sharpen your search skills although you might find that some excellent opportunities may not be in these settings. Be sure to give serious consideration to any employer from whom you request information.

Realistic   As we face difficult times, we can *refocus* to see the good
and   in what we have faced in the people near us. We can
Optimistic   be optimistic *and* realistic as we look to the future.

On some difficult days, I have awakened thinking that I would like to write some acquaintances to tell them how much I think of them and how much their special qualities have meant to me. Everyone can think of these same kind of people if they take time to reflect.

SIGNING ON THE DOTTED LINE

Success-what is it for you?

If you have reached that time when you have decided on a position and the employer has decided on you, you may have to sign tax forms, retirement plan papers, insurance information, and other assorted materials. You will not likely understand all of it, but you should make an effort to learn of your benefits through employee-orientation meetings or individual conferences.

Success   Is success a mountain peak to be reached or an attainable feeling of satisfaction? If it is a peak, do you have to come down after you reach it? My simple definition of success is "being happy with yourself."

As you have read through this booklet, you have had the chance to reflect upon your own ideas of success. The booklet has been written to show *how* important *a career relates to* one's *life*. More importantly though, it, hopefully, has tried to encourage the readers to see that *how one leads his or her life* will have the most to do with the career in which one embarks. A daily effort to be happy with yourself and others may make this process happen.

Reflecting on the following may again let you consider their importance for you.

You will define success for yourself. Others will offer their expectations for you, but you will ultimately decide how you and your conscience will mesh. Some people's "conscience" or their perception of "what is right and wrong" will differ, and therefore, what makes them happy will vary. If your conscience includes an *honest respect* for other's rights, then your happiness will not interfere with another's life.

Seeing the Best in All Things and in All Events

Not with an attitude where "everything will be okay" but with a realistic view of life, can you

1. Go to a class or a meeting with the attitude that your presence can make a difference?
2. Artistically appreciate the varying shades of gray on an *overcast* or otherwise dreary day?
3. Consider that ceremonies are not *just* gatherings but possible *beginnings* for future greatness?

If you find yourself being critical much of your waking hours, you might want to refocus and ask yourself, what is it that you have done to help the situation?

If you criticize a lot of things, then first take time to be critical of yourself.

Do not believe or let your job, a computer, or any inanimate thing be the ultimate in your life.

TO KEEP A JOB, MAKE TIME FOR YOURSELF

Managing your time

Make Time   What do you do with your day and your time? Taking time to plan and consider your options *will* be invaluable.

Schedule   Make a schedule (*only as a guide*) of things you do on a regular basis. A personal calendar is usually found near most successful people.

As You
Begin
Work or
If You Are
Looking
for Work

1. List and prioritize your responsibilities.
2. Learn how to say *no* appropriately.
3. In tasks of lesser importance, perfection may not be required.
4. Do not keep going over the same issue. Write down concerns and make decisions.
5. Organize your work day and your work area.
6. Do not waste time complaining or running someone down.
7. Do not try to do too much in one day!
8. Do not go to the extreme and get *too* organized.

Numbers 1, 2, 3, and 5 are paraphrased and reprinted with permission from the book *How to Get Control of Your Time and Life*, copyright by Alan Lakein and published by David McKay Co. Inc.

Take time to think, it is the source of power
Take time to play, it is the secret to perpetual youth
Take time to read, it is the fountain of wisdom
Take time to pray, it is the greatest power on earth
Take time to love and be loved, it is a gift to be shared
Take time to be friendly, it is the road to happiness
Take time to laugh, it is the music of the soul
Take time to give, it is too short a day to be selfish
Take time to work, it is the price of success.

—Anonymous
From a North Carolina Agricultural
Extension Service Publication

*Make time and effort to get rid of any bad feelings
toward others so new growth can begin. Time may heal
wounds, but we can and must learn to live with scars
as we forgive those who may have done us wrong.*

*It is not good to phone as a place is opening or closing, and
it is not good to call someone at home unless they offer.*

*When you give honestly, the more it appears that
there are good things enough for all of us.*

UNDERSTANDING WORK SITUATIONS

People Management

People Management

A GOOD MANAGER OF PEOPLE IS GENERALLY A LIKABLE PERSON. Some observations and qualities about persons who have exhibited outstanding skills and abilities in my life are as follows:

1. They let each person know where he or she stands. This gives emotional stability to all, so others do not have to guess.
2. They allow people the opportunity to work to the limit of their abilities.
3. They are supportive—they know how and when to give credit.
4. They let people know of changes in advance and of when they will affect them. One of many fine professors I had, Dr. Frank Fuller offered these first four statements in a class.
5. They do not smother talent. They are not threatened by people with strengths that they do not have but allow the person's talent to blend with their skills.
6. They do not expect the worst from people or new situations.
7. They do not judge others on that which they cannot see. They trust their employees until their employees prove untrustworthy.
8. They recognize their own weaknesses.

NO EMPLOYER OR BOSS CAN BE EXPECTED TO DO ALL
THESE THINGS—DO NOT EXPECT THEM TO BE PERFECT
UNLESS THEY CAN EXPECT THE SAME OF YOU!

A fine gardener may transfer some of his skills to be a good manager or supervisor:	**Some things a good manager might do:**
Get certified seed	Pick good employees
Select good soil	Have a job site ready
Weed when necessary	Clear distractions
Add correct amounts of fertilizer without killing crops	Give appropriate doses of praise
Does not stand over crop and block natural sunlight	Give people room
Water as necessary	Don't let possibilities dry up

There are very few perfect bosses or mates, but there are many pleasant working environments and many happy marriages.

Appreciate the differences in people. Differences never provide an excuse for lack of courtesy.

No one likes to work where their work is never quite good enough.

V

VIEW YOURSELF AS IMPORTANT BUT REPLACEABLE

Viewing yourself and others

You Are Unique

Even though you bring a unique set of experiences and ideas to a work setting, there are always others who might fill in for you and possibly do things differently and possibly better. It is probably obvious to you as you have read or skimmed earlier sections that your *success* in work will depend on your personality, how you think, and how you live your life.

How Do You View Others?

The way you view others will tell a lot about how you view yourself. What do you first observe in others? One of the biggest mistakes we make is to *underestimate one another*. If someone could point out your unlimited potential, you would not believe it. All people have unique and special qualities. Let people discover your talents or special qualities.

Private Time

Allow for some private time to reflect on your qualities and those of others. Essentially, do not be quick to criticize. ALLOW A PERSON SOME BAD DAYS AND IGNORE WHAT MAY BE MOODINESS.

Criticism

The person who is critical will be the most replaceable. The person critical of former employees will most often soon be complaining about a new situation.

Values   What is it that you really feel is important? If it is material things, then your possessions will lose their appeal if there is no one with whom to share them. Is a good, satisfying life your goal? Is a healthy body what you most desire? Will financial rewards take care of your needs? Do you want to be appreciated and loved?

To be appreciated and loved, show appreciation and love.

If you do not know how to show these, then learn about them through the example of another.

To Accept and 1. Communicate—remember though that just because
Appreciate   you send a message (or a letter), there is no guarantee
Others   that it is received. Try and *let* the recipient respond.
2. Just because you have knowledge of something, do not expect everyone to know or understand it.
3. No one likes the attitude of a know-it-all. It sometimes is important to listen twice as much as you talk.
4. Do not assume that the other person automatically understands what you have tried to communicate.
5. It is much too easy to blame others for your misfortunes. Few people will take responsibility or accept the idea that they were wrong.

Do not expect others to accept you if you cannot accept those you encounter.

Life loses meaning if there is no one who cares about you but yourself.

W

WAGES AND WORKING TOGETHER

Salary

1. Do you know what the starting salary has been for your desired position previously?

2. Will you take a job because it has a significantly high salary range?

3. Can you accept that others hired with your same background may be making more than you do?

Many factors must be taken in consideration when discussing salary. Some factors that may be considered are:

*   Health Benefits

*   Will your work be appreciated?

*   Is your job basically secure?

*   Will your work be interesting?

WORKING TOGETHER

If you are going to work with people, lead or be part of a group, or if you go to meetings, then you can make a difference as you think about your responsibility in the particular setting to:

1. Help determine or point out realistic goals for the group.

2. GIVE PEOPLE ROOM—If you are the leader and have **someone** who is **self-motivated**, then do not ask a lot of them. They will most often do more than you could ask if you will give them flexibility. If you put out too many expectations for them, they may be resentful and do only the minimum to complete a task.

3. Do not drag things out. Always try to find a way to end meetings five minutes before people may expect them to finish.

4. In the announcements of meetings, share general topics to be covered or an agenda so people can prepare.

5. As a boss or co-worker, one wrongful thing you might do is to ask to see someone at a given date and time **without explanation** of what you hope to accomplish. Take time to tell an employee or friend that you want to meet at 2:30 about _____> This way they can bring the appropriate information and frame of mind to the meeting.

6. If two people are to talk at a meeting allow 30 minutes, one person can do best with 14 minutes and most groups function best in less than 45-minute time frames.

Do not stop just child abuse—work in your lives to end people abuse.

Do not infer to others, "Why have you not done anything in that area?
If you must ask, sincerely inquire "Is there anything
that I might do to assist in that area?
To suggest to someone that something is not being done
will most often put the person(s) on the defensive.

Most people do not mind hard work if they like it.

Consider how you might make your work or studies more enjoyable.

X

X-RAY YOUR OWN WORK SITUATION—IS MORE SCHOOLING NECESSARY?

Is more education necessary

Is the last place you left better off because you were there or because you are gone?

Is your world, your work, or the people that you have known better off because of things that you have done?

Happy in Your Work and Life? If you are *happy* in your work and in your life, then you can probably check the following as they apply to you:

1. Do not live in the past.
2. Do not try to change the unchangeable.
3. Believe in something bigger than yourself.
4. Do not expect too much of yourself. As you do a job, you realize that similar situations will likely occur again a year from now.
5. Recognize raw deals or, at least, learn from them.
6. Do not feel hostile toward life and other people.
7. Be forgiving of others' weaknesses and wrongdoings.
8. Do not try to do too much. If you try to do everything, people will let you.
9. Have you received appreciation without any forced expectations of another?
10. Know how to show appreciation.

More Schooling Necessary? We will function best if we adopt an attitude of being always willing to learn. If formal schooling is possibly needed, then *ask questions with no obligation* to

schools in your community,
online instruction,
community colleges or technical universities or colleges.
specific departments, and
graduate or professional schools (your company might pay).

In your own situation   In your job or school situation now, can you say that you have been
1. supportive of your employer or school,
2. free from spreading wrong information,
3. careful not to align with anyone too soon,
4. respectful of coworkers and the way they have done things,
5. able to avoid office politics and recognize that some work days will not be as enjoyable as others, and
6. trustworthy and honest in all your dealings?

Sincere and kind words can make a lasting impression. At appropriate times, they will be more valuable than any amount of money.

Always being right will lead to always being lonely.

The person who has the most success in a job search (or a relationship) is one who can think, understand, and appreciate the perspectives of others involved.

Y

YOUR JOB, YOUR CAREER, AND YOUR LIFE

Build on a solid foundation

A *job* may just be a position or a way to earn money.

A *career* will involve your total way of *life*.

Consider this analogy about *jobs* and a *career*.

THE PROCESS OF LOOKING FOR A JOB OR A CAREER
IS MUCH LIKE BUILDING A HOUSE.

On what *foundation* are you planning to build?

Has your land surface been graded and surveyed?
Have you looked at yourself and gotten rid of your rough spots?

Who have been the *suppliers* of your building materials?

Have you chosen quality and reliable suppliers?
Have you chosen the most appropriate
educational institution for your study?

Who have been the financial backers of your endeavors?

Have you established your credit worthiness in past dealings?
Have you shown appreciation to those who have
given you a chance to prove yourself?

What tools will you need? Is customized work necessary?

Do you have the skills or training required by those in the field?
Do you have specific skills an employer should know about?

Will your *blueprint* provide the guide for future work?

Does your plan meet the standards for construction?
Have you done sufficient planning before you start to build?

Before starting to build, some careful planning is required to have a structure to last over time. With this in mind, one must reflect on their own *foundation, suppliers, financial backers, tools,* and *blueprint.* Recognizing this process will help insure more solid construction and a better structure in which one can live.

People can do almost anything they set their minds on if they have the proper motivation and if they can focus in on what they really want to do.

You can learn something from anyone.

Be your own friend first.

Z

ZERO IN ON BEING HAPPY WITH YOURSELF

A Life With Others

If you have chosen to start reviewing this booklet here or if you have now skimmed it once, then please recognize what is involved in printing my thoughts and observations in this way.

Our brains supposedly record everything, but how we make use of the materials stored away will vary with each person.

My eyes and ears have been fortunate to have learned from many teachers, relatives, ministers, friends, and acquaintances. From a combination of what they have shared, this pamphlet is the result.

My personal *thoughts*, *quotes*, or *observations* at the bottom of the pages were inspired by many people throughout my life. I have jotted down the ideas over the past twenty-five years and used them where I saw an opportunity under the A–Z sections.

Anyone who reviews *this collection* of observations about careers and life can see that my belief is that what you do today can greatly influence tomorrow. That is why the emphasis has certainly been on the individual and *how one chooses* to live his or her life. Goodness does seem to return to those who are willing to give first of themselves.

Recognizing that there will always be powers or events that exist and that we can't control, we must try to do what we have learned is the right and best thing to do.

We can't expect to change other people or make them believe as we do; we can't expect to make an employer see as we see. We can only prepare in appropriate ways, and then, we seem to often evolve or fall into the work that we most deserve.

Find peace with yourself and in your search. As you learn and mature in job-hunting techniques, you will see that there are good things enough for all of us who live honestly.

Remember that we can always learn and that everyone has something to share.

If at first you do not succeed, you might try again, but don't become a pest and drag anything out. People like to end things that do not seem to have a remote chance for a future.

Keep your possibilities open, and you will discover your opportunities as you live and learn.

In the last episode of a most famous TV series *M*A*S*H* on CBS television, Colonel Potter said to a very career-oriented Hot Lips a powerful statement that we all might consider as we prepare and establish ourselves in a career. He said simply, "I know that you have got your career in order, but don't forget to have a happy life along the way!" I hope that you will

Act after obtaining accurate information,
Begin and look at your areas of interest,
Create opportunities to learn from others,
Determine your strengths and not just your weaknesses,
Evaluate your life and not just your strife,
Find your meaning through sufficient gleaning,
Gather information and avoid misinformation,
Have a good and satisfying life,
Instill a positive attitude for yourself,
Joke when others can appreciate humor,
Keep a generous and pure heart,
Leap over obstacles or at least learn from them,
Move with confidence and courage,
Never step on others who are down,
Open your mind for inevitable changes,
Protect yourself with foresight,
Question in ways that do not threaten,
Resist temptations that seem too good to be true,
Stand fast to the principles of right,
Take time to learn from the young and old,
Understand those people with whom you work,
View yourself and recognize your potential,
Watch out for others who need your help,
X-ray your own life first,
Yearn for what is best for all, and
Zero in on being happy with yourself.

—JRW

DR. JAMES "JIM" ROGERS WESTMORELAND

Doctorate of Education in the Department of Occupational Education

   North Carolina State University, Raleigh, North Carolina

   Dissertation—"The Importance of Career Planning and Placement Services Within the Public Universities of North Carolina"

   4.0 GPA in all coursework, Phi Kappa Phi Honor Society

   Phi Delta Kappa Educational Honor Society

   American Society of Training and Development—Research Triangle Park Chapter

Master of Arts in Adult Education—Emphasis on Career Development

   Completed while working full-time at East Carolina University, May 1981

   Kappa Delta Pi Education Honor Society Adult Education Association—ECU Chapter

Master of Arts in Counselor Education, East Carolina University, August 1975

   Became certified by the State of North Carolina

Bachelor of Arts-Political Science/Business minor, ECU

SAMPLING OF CAREER SERVICES–RELATED OFFICES VISITED

University of Hawaii	UCLA	Tennessee	NCSU	MIT
University of Washington	MIT	Georgia	NCA&T	Auburn
Harvard	Yale	Georgia State	UNC–CH	Clemson
Florida State	Princeton	Miami	UNC–G	Vanderbilt
Orleans, France	UVA	Richmond	Ga Tech	UNC–C

SAMPLING OF MAJOR PUBLICATIONS AND PRESENTATIONS

cAreer BasiCs Copyrighted 1996, ABC's of Career Preparation Copyrighted 1983, a workbook or guide for job searchers covering self-assessment, study skills, has been sold for high schools, community colleges, and universities

National Association of Student-Employment Administrators, November 1984.

North Carolina 4-H Agents Convention, Nags Head, North Carolina, October 1986.

Presentation of Developing a Professional Portfolio

"Training and Education Needed in the World of Work in a Changing Society" for 150 North Carolina guidance counselors for the UNC General Administration

"Rejections Can Lead to More Success" in Career Opportunities, *Raleigh News and Observer*, May 1986.

Speaker for Community Groups (Rotary Club, BPW), high schools, TV news stories

Speaker for Thomas Nelson/ Varsity Publishers Sales Meeting, Columbus, Georgia, July 1993.

OTHER RELEVANT WORK EXPERIENCE

Associate Dean, ECU College of Business

Director and Assistant Director of Career Services

Division of Student Life

Division of Continuing Education – East Carolina University

Team-Taught Distance Education, an adult-education class, Summer 1993.

Assisted with counselor, education-graduate classes at Fort Bragg, Summer/Fall 1975, 1980.

Assistant for Elementary Guidance Workshop

Aycock Junior High School (Grades 7, 8, 9), Graduate Internship

North Carolina Department of Revenue—Ad Valorem Tax Division

Office of the Attorney General of North Carolina

PROFESSIONAL ORGANIZATIONS

College Placement Council Institutional Representative—Attended San Francisco National and Las Vegas National Meetings; Southern College Placement Association; Attended meetings in Orlando, Nashville, Charlotte, Atlanta, Mobile, Served on Ethics, Legal, and Governmental Affairs Committee.

North Carolina Placement Association / Honorary lifetime membership as NCACE

Historian—two terms, Awards Committee, Directory Committee

NC Career Development Association/ NC Vocational Guidance Association (two conferences)

External Involvement: For community

- Workforce Development of Pitt Co. (continued to help review proposal which received renewal of $160,000 grant)

- Served on Chamber of Commerce TECH PREP Committee, served with business and educational leaders

- Speaker for local organizations—Rose High's Transition to College Program

- American Society for Training and Development—meetings

- Developed contacts in the business community through memberships in the Pitt County Quality Network

- Traveled to various businesses at own expense (Nortel and Altec)

Internal Involvement (on campus): For other divisions/departments

In addition to presentations to clubs, classes, and organizations

- Served on the Faculty Senate Career Education Committee

- Led two programs at prospective "Teaching Fellows" Conference

- Served as Alumni Weekend Tour guide (highlight—US senator Robert Morgan as guest)

- Coordinated the *Pirate Alumni Network* with Institutional Advancement, Developed new packets ready for presentation to alumni chapter presidents

- Planned and implemented successful Business Career Day

- Coordinated Health Career Day

- Arranged and handled all details for Education Career Day

- Served as consultant to English Department on their Information Exchange Day

- Provided support for second Science Career Day

- Obtained computers for student internet access in media room

- Coordinated class visits and presented to almost all English 3880 Technical Writing classes

- Participated in minority open house, university fairs

- Participated in major's/minor's fair

Internally (within own division)

- Led group to have 100 percent participation in state-employee campaign

- Participated on search committees, interviewed candidates for all other campus positions

- Staff, participated in Midnight Madness, Mardi Gras, Funnel of Obsession

- Served on Quality Committee for Division of Student Life to provide workshops on quality awareness and to develop a survey of quality for the division

- Presented résumé/job-search class in cultural center

Internally (within career services)

- Worked with staff and Office of Research and Testing in a "for follow-up" survey

- For all Graduates—developed questionnaire, mailed surveys, and wrote report of results

- Continued effort to develop "Career-Education Coordinators"

- Coordinated the meetings and development of "Career-Services Representatives

- Continued rewrite of office-and-student operational manuals, prepared extra correspondence

- Worked collaboratively with staff, faculty, and other departments in presenting workshops, programs, and outreach activities

- Provided professional, congenial service to employers recruiting on campus

- Continued programs on "Preparing for Career Days" and "Professionalism in the Workplace: Making the Transition," presented to several groups

- Established stronger relationships with faculty in business, industrial technology, and communication department

- Re-established and developed relationships with faculty in human environmental sciences, education, sociology, decision sciences

- Presented "Combination Program of Orientation / Résumé / Interview Sessions" to all nursing seniors, OT, CSDI, HIMA, and most physical-therapy graduates

- Held numerous orientation/registration sessions every week

- Offered almost weekly résumé-and-interviewing workshops

- Scheduled all workshops in conjunction with other programs and activities

- Offered MACES (Major And Career Exploration System) connected to Home Page for access by students, academic advisors, and other faculty to assist students in learning about career options.

- Continued in receivership agreement with Jobtrak so that employers can select ECU

- Worked to consistently maintain excellent rapport with students and employers through effective communication and professional service.

- Wrote and submitted announcements of programs and special events

- Coordinated Pirate Alumni Network correspondence within Career Services

"Best to you in your search and discoveries"

Thank you for sharing this with a friend or counselor or mentor!